The Lost Letters of Mileva

M. MIRANDA MALONEY

Copyright © 2014 M. Miranda Maloney

All rights reserved. No part of this book may be reproduced in any manner without the express written consent of the Publisher, except in the case of brief excerpts in critical reviews or articles. All inquiries should be addressed to: Pandora Lobo Estepario Productions, 1239 N. Greenview Ave. Chicago, IL 60642

ISBN: 194085606X
ISBN-13: 978-1-940856-06-3

Library of Congress Control Number: 2014904739

DEDICATION

To Daniel Chacon and Dolores Dorantes

CONTENTS

One
*Sustain me with flowers, surround me with apples,
for I'm dying of love.*
—Song of Songs, 2:5

I wait through winter	1
We are blind and delicate	2
Don't insist. Spring is in clear view	3
"Mileva," you write,	4
Take heart	5
I set up equations	6
Capillarity, Beloved.	7
My belly fills with you	8

Two
I die because I do not die
—Teresa de Avila

Arthur Miller writes	11
I sit by a window watching	12
We have become nothing	13
What you have heard is true	14
It is difficult for bodies to act	15
He stays home tonight	16
If only he would declare	17
It's March	18
Lola	19
All speculation	20
I miss the days of sailing	21

Three
May Be / I had to / forget how…
—Dolores Dorantes (trans. by Jen Hofer)

I'm thinking of body	23
I spread	24
From this window	25
Our mouths divide with apologies	26
I'm set to dry and he begins	27

ACKNOWLEDGMENTS

Grateful acknowledgments to Dolores Dorantes whose work inspired these letters, and for her editorial comment. In similar fashion, to my husband for his correspondence during his deployment to Iraq. Some of his words are netted in these letters.

ONE

Sustain me with flowers, surround me with apples,
for I'm dying with love.

—*Song of Songs 2:5*

1

I wait through winter buried under Zurich's snow.
Warm in gloves
of memory. White snow betrays
the melancholy of my days. Grey.
In spring, when I return to you,
it will be with my deformed love, venturing into
your universe.
Your back bent over a book, and trains
in their passing will remind you
I will be grazing
in your fields.
You'll lift your eyes, recall my olive skin, my lips
purring against yours.
Beloved, the days bleed dark.
Tulips grow at the edge of the rain.

2

We are blind and delicate.
We try to take back our words,
to unravel our time together, untangle
our language of stars,
but the force
of attraction is inevitable,
as is the last breath.

I wait and dance with my agony.
Cold in bed. In the morning,
the coffee is lukewarm in my throat.

3

Don't insist. Spring is in clear view.
I am an insomniac fool.
I think of her, the one who breast-fed you,
the one who tenderly steals
your eyes away from mine.
I see your bohemian
poverty outside her rooms.
How she cries for you.
I am from the land of pepper.
You are light, the bulb.
Women like me, she says,
are thieves. We leave
nothing behind.

4

"Mileva," you write, "this ordinary man needs you."
Am I lovely, my love? Does my exoticness excite you?
Or do you need me for my theory of functions?
Then why I'm drowning in your want
for solitude more brilliant than a thousand suns.
What can be clearer than this woman
who desires to rest her head upon
your delicate chest?

5

Take heart. Heidelberg is laced in moods, swallowed in moonless nights. I retreat to your letters like a feeding bottle. I am obedient to your biding when you ask
I should write only when I'm bored. My waiting has been in vain.
I pick up this pen. Make love to you.

6

I set up equations, differentiate, substitute. Peace skirts
over me like the din
of clocks announcing the hours, and I yield
to the memory of your arms, my hands
over your hard stomach. The maple trees above
quiver from our breathing.
I could go on all night mathematically trying
in vain an equation for this void.

Answer me, my darling. What takes so long?
Tell me you feel the same.

My little boots wait for you at the door.

Capillarity, Beloved. We must fall and rise in body with our insanity spread in sand. *Remember your hand to mine, strangers at the edge of water.*

How we fall like dropping stars.
How we rise fiery as sun
in an endless Monet's stroke.
How we break our hearts over and over in the distance, diving into black holes.
How we rise again, putting down roots.

8

My belly fills with you.
Your spirit into my body, your
history, your dreams.
In the thread of light,
I devour repetition. Spit it out.
The sun, our sun remains only.
I wait like a trembling leaf
       for your return.
Wait, dying with love,
a piece of you growing inside
of me.

I want to see you.

TWO

I die because I do not die
　　　　—Teresa de Avila

Arthur Miller writes in his treatise of *Space, Time, and Beauty*, that I am a sulking wife, and it is no wonder Albert spends eight hours of free "mischief," plus Sunday, at the Patent Office. All this talk of electrodynamics of moving bodies and ether-drift strains our marriage. The only movement and drift in Albert's calculations will be me. Lola, I'm so lonely. Bern is covered in snow.

I sit by a window watching a tiny bird unravel from his shell. Hans Albert is colicky, and I can't keep the dinner table uncluttered. Last night, Albert worked on his mathematical formulae long into the night. The smoke of cheap, Swiss cigars filled the room. How easily he detaches from the merely personal, and I am his little sounding board. Bubbles, Lola, tiny bubbles, many bubbles escaping from the bird's tiny beak. There is so much pain in the first breath of life.

We have become nothing. I tell me soul,
do not be foolish. Love cannot be forsaken
unless love forsakes
first. No one loses you, only the one
who leaves you willingly.

Everyday he plans his departure.
Everyday he tells her he'll be there soon.

What you have heard is true, Lola. This Dollie Affair is almost dead. Nothing remains of Dollie and Johnnie. Yet, the mountains do not disappeared, as a Cézanne painting at the end of the artist's diseased eye; the mountains are there: implacable and adamant. He is right. The mind invents the form and there are so many other ways of seeing. If he could only see my emptiness showing through. The light that has outrun me, us, would he reconsider?

Imagine corks floating in a pond, drifting apart.

It is difficult for bodies to act on one another at a distance. The ether is undetectable, and he retreats from me, determined to measure its presence. It is there, I tell him. Look closer; envision what brought us together. The irony is living in a small space where bodies attract and repel each other. He has not touched me in months.

He stays home tonight, forgetting the inefficient Besso. I hear he has no talent for writing patent appraisals, and if it weren't for Albert's intervention, old Haller would have fired him long ago. But, happiness, my dearest! Albert and I talked like old times: of electrodynamics, molecular forces, surface phenomena, dissociation, Newtonian physics, Poincaré, and Lorentz. We drink tea, eat sausages, and even Hans Albert sleeps quietly. Afterward, we watch the stars over Bern, magnificently blue. Later, Albert says to me, "They were misled by their intuition." "Who?" I asked. "Poincaré and Lorentz, us."

If only he would declare light is both wave and particle, we would have peace in this house. At night, my coverlet is my anger. I douse it with tears. It is useless to encounter the gaze of a fantasist. Albert clings with great love to his science, and I have given so much. Whatever became of my poor Leiserl? Has she run into my own fate?

It's March, and I have seen the last snowfall. Tomorrow the train departs for Novi Sad, and I will be waiting at the station. It has been useless to hint and hope for signs. Truth is not possible between lovers who ceased to be long ago anything but floating bodies in a shared space. More than anything, I have always envied his freedom.

Lola, I have lost everything that matters. Hans Albert is lonely and bitter. Eduard is a schizophrenic, and I, long ago lost my scientific aspiration. Yet, life is tolerable, and their father shares his wealth. It is time to recalibrate, and seize a second chance. The stars, after all, are not where they are supposed to be, and the universe is not static, but try telling that to the old hag!

All speculation, of course, my dearest, Lola, forgive
me for the infrared night scopes, the grasping hand,
the depth perception, color vision, night's versatility.
These things I seek from desperation like touch. My
only enemy for staying here among the dying is
gravity. I am storm tossed and he is my tiller.

I miss the days of sailing in Lake Zurich. The days of hiking up the Alps, and he, always he, asking, "How's your little throat?"

THREE

May Be

*I had to forget
how…*

—*Dolores Dorantes*

(trans. by Jen Hofer)

I'm thinking of body— tailored
insomnia in the eyelids. The study of
motherhood across the belly   lies don't fade
                              but widened

The back calcified
by the epidural choice of
three babies. Mid-life and empty-nested,
time craved in the neck

The edit begins
Love everything
Love nothing

I spread
my age like autumn
under trees—

color hardens, shape softens

Wind carries everything
Take me

From this window:
Organic oranges and
conclusions   piled rubble
and conclusions
            At rising a rasping
bird on tangled vines   an old man gutting
out his throat through
a screen door across the courtyard

an open doorway nothing but bent backs   a sad hello
over cactus wire
around their gardens   delicate visits
of anxiety our ceaseless skinning of

Our mouths divide with apologies
now lies
now nothing but forests
    between us
and in his sky a grape
is an act

I'm set to dry and he begins
to grow

with
of,
the of
grows with fanfare

I, condemn
       my violence, the sun, a snow-capped war—

There was a story here

Publisher

Pandora lobo estepario Productions
http://www.loboestepario.com/press

Front Cover Photograph:
Model: Alida Bosco
Photograph: Miguel López Lemus©

Made in the USA
Columbia, SC
03 February 2022